Mary Alice   4/06

Peace be in your garden
   AND YOUR HEART

thanks for EVERYTHING!

Nancy Portugal Jamello

1

POTTED PLANT
ORGANIC CARE

THIRD EDITION

by

JODY MAIN & NANCY PORTUGAL

Wild Horses Potted Plant

PALO ALTO · EUREKA

3

Library of Congress Cataloging in Publication Data

Main, Jody,
    Potted plant organic care.

    (Living on our planet)
    Previous ed. published under title: Potted plant
organic care handbook.
    1. House plants. 2. Indoor gardening.
3. Organic gardening. I. Portugal, Nancy,
joint author. II. Title.
SB419.M263 1980   635.9'65   79-22173
ISBN 0-9601088-7-4

REPRINTED 1980
Printed in U.S.A

COORDINATED BY PAM PORTUGAL

Wild Horse Potted Plant
PUBLISHERS
HOME GROWN BOOKS™

in the ~~~~~~

226 HAMIL~~~~~~   ~~A. 94301

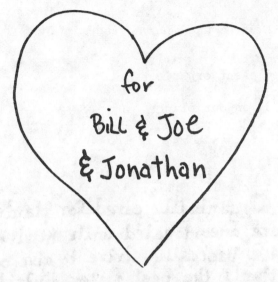

for
Bill & Joe
& Jonathan

EDITED BY —— Annette DAVIS & PRP

BOUND BY EUREKA PRINTING CO.
TEXT PRINTED BY ARCATA UNION
COVER PRINTED BY ARTCRAFT
Music BY —— The RAP CITY BAND

· CONTRIBUTORS ·

THANK YOU TO OUR family & friends for their
encouragement & inspiration. and for their HELP
WRITING and HAND·LETTERING: JAN & MARV ADELMAN,
DAVE & AMY BOISSEVAIN, JESSIE BORG, JIM BIBBLER,
ROGER & SASHA DAVIS, LINDA CORBETT, ECOLOGY ACTION,
SHEILA SCHENCK HALCOMB, JOE JAMELLO, BILL MAIN,
DOTTIE, GENE & THE PETER PORTUGALS, SUZANNA WYNKOOP,
DAN & GLORIA & JERRY SHANE, & JOHN COGGINS...

Organically cared for plants are ones treated with kindness. We basically strive to give our plants the best water, nutrition, and environment we can.

We try to make our plants comfortable in our homes.

Organic care is a loving, rewarding & simple way to care for your house-plants. From this volume we hope you acquire a genuine understanding of plants & the organic method.

♡

contents:

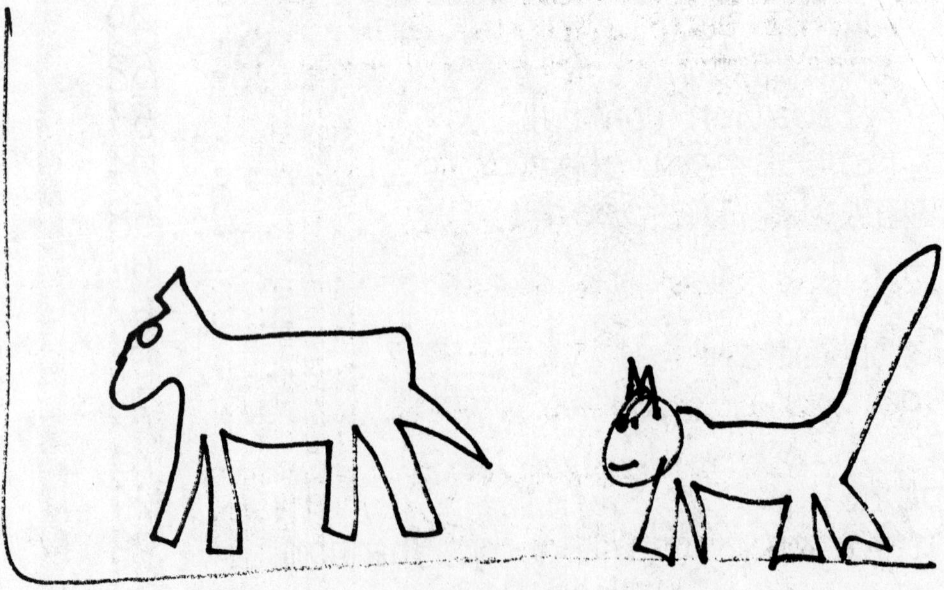

♥ INTRODUCTION ♥

living with your Plants

Houseplants are living things. They need to eat drink and rest. They need the sunlight and warmth and fresh air. They need to be kept healthy and they can't do it on their own.

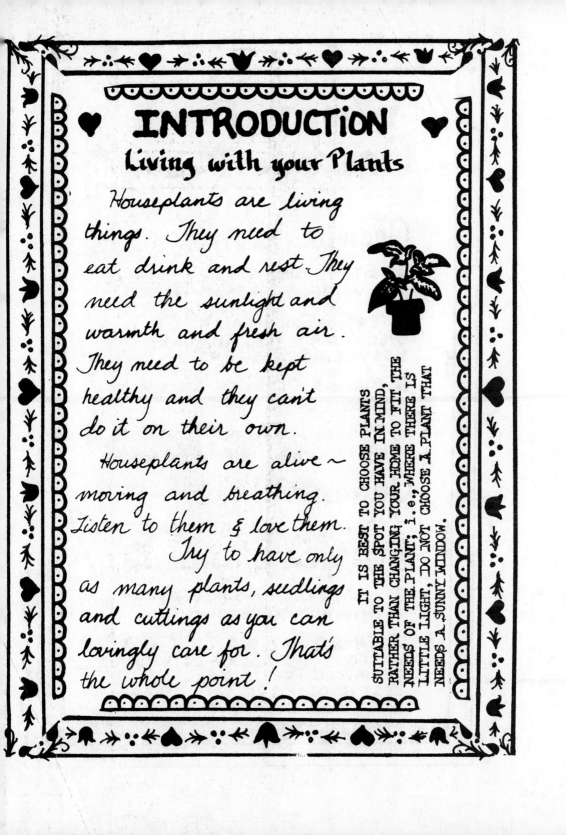

Houseplants are alive ~ moving and breathing. Listen to them & love them.

Try to have only as many plants, seedlings and cuttings as you can lovingly care for. That's the whole point!

IT IS BEST TO CHOOSE PLANTS SUITABLE TO THE SPOT YOU HAVE IN MIND, RATHER THAN CHANGING YOUR HOME TO FIT THE NEEDS OF THE PLANT; i.e., WHERE THERE IS LITTLE LIGHT, DO NOT CHOOSE A PLANT THAT NEEDS A SUNNY WINDOW.

WHAT DOES ORGANIC MEAN?

ORGANIC LIVING—

1. STYLE OF BEING, A WAY OF COPING, A LEARNING PROCESS.

2. EATING FOR HEALTH, CO-OPERATING WITH NATURE, RECYCLING WASTES.

3. MAKING DO WITH LESS & ENJOYING IT MORE.

4. HAVING REGARD FOR OUR PLANET AS A WHOLE.

ORGANIC FOOD—

1. CONTAINS NO CHEMICAL PRESERVATIVES, FLAVORS, OR OTHER ARTIFICIAL INGREDIENTS.

2. HAS BEEN SUBJECTED TO MINIMAL PROCESSING.

3. TRANSPORTED & CULTIVATED WITHOUT THE USE OF INORGANIC CHEMICAL FERTILIZERS OR PESTICIDES—THE SOIL BEING ENRICHED BY ADDED HUMUS.

4. ANIMAL PRODUCTS GROWN WITH ORGANIC FEED & NOT TREATED WITH GROWTH STIMULENTS, ANTIBIOTICS, OR HORMONES.

ORGANIC PLANT CARE

1. CARING FOR HOUSE PLANTS BY CREATING AN ENVIRONMENT AS CLOSE TO THEIR NATURAL OUTDOOR COMMUNITY AS YOU CAN.

2. TREATING PLANTS WITH KINDNESS- ⓐ GOOD WATER, ENVIRONMENT & NATURAL FOOD (ORGANIC MATTER - e.g. FISH EMULSION) ⓑ KEEPING PLANTS CLEAN & PEST FREE WITHOUT THE USE OF CHEMICAL POISONS.

3. LEARNING TO CARE FOR ANOTHER LIVING THING WITH BASIC NEEDS SIMILAR TO OUR OWN.

4. MAKING PLANTS COMFORTABLE IN OUR HOMES.

Some of These ideas are From:
"ORGANIC GARDENING & FARMING MAG."
NOV. 1974 & FEB 1975

in nature - plants get the water they need from rain, streams, springs and creeks.

Moisture is retained in the soil for a long time because of nature's way of mulching

Indoors - you are totally in charge of the amount of water your plants get.

EGG WATER

Watering

All your plants will not need watering at the same time. To test if your plant needs water... poke your finger 1" down. If the soil is dry - your plant is probably thirsty. After awhile you will be able (on some plants) to simply touch or look at the soil's surface and just know. ♥ How often you need to water your plants depends on: the SEASON, POT, SOIL and HUMIDITY.

the Seasons

WE FOUND THAT SOME PLANTS NEEDING WATER ONLY EVERY OTHER WEEK DURING THE WINTER NEEDED WATER TWICE A WEEK DURING SUMMER.

<u>RESTING</u> - DURING THE FALL AND WINTER MONTHS, MOST PLANTS DON'T REQUIRE FREQUENT WATERING BECAUSE THEY ARE NOT GROWING VERY MUCH. THE SOIL STAYS MOIST LONGER BECAUSE IT IS USUALLY COOL, DARK AND HUMID.

<u>GROWING</u> - DURING SPRING AND SUMMER, PLANTS NEED BIG DRINKS BECAUSE THEY ARE GROWING ALOT.... AND... BECAUSE THE SOIL MOISTURE EVAPORATES QUICKLY IN THE DRY HEAT.

fall

Winter

Spring

Summer

13

POTS

UNGLAZED CLAY POTS ARE VERY POROUS & HOLD MOISTURE FOR A SHORTER PERIOD OF TIME THAN GLAZED CLAY POTS. PLASTIC POTS HOLD MOISTURE THE LONGEST BECAUSE THE ONLY PLACE FOR THE WATER TO ESCAPE IS OUT THE TOP. TRYING TO KEEP A SMALL CLAY POT MOIST DURING THE SUMMER IS SOMETIMES IMPOSSIBLE. LARGE PLASTIC POTS DURING THE WINTER MAY KEEP YOUR PLANTS TOO SOGGY. YOU HAVE TO BE THE JUDGE. GENERALLY, THE LARGER THE POT, THE LESS FRE- QUENT WATERINGS IT WILL NEED.———

SOIL

——— DIFFERENT SOILS RETAIN MOISTURE FOR DIFFERENT LENGTHS OF TIME. SOIL HIGH IN HUMUS WILL HOLD MOISTURE MUCH LONGER THAN SOIL LACKING IN HUMUS BUT HAVING A HIGH SAND CONTENT. THE IDEA IS TO GET A NICE EVEN MIXTURE. IT'S VERY EASY TO MAKE UP A POTTING MIX — JUST FOLLOW YOUR NOSE AND ADD WHAT LOOKS AND FEELS GOOD. WE RECOMMEND USING COMPOST FOR YOUR POTTING MIX. IF YOUR COMPOST BATCH IS HIGHLY CONCENTRATED WITH KITCHEN WASTE AND IS VERY POTENT, ADD SOME SOIL, HUMUS AND SAND UNTIL IT FEELS RIGHT. MANY PACKAGED SOILS ARE VERY GOOD AND CONVENIENT TO USE. MOST IMPORTANT IS THAT YOUR POTTING MIX IS NUTRITIOUS AND HAS GOOD TEXTURE FOR GOOD DRAINAGE AND WATER DISTRIBUTION.

14

✣ humidity ✣

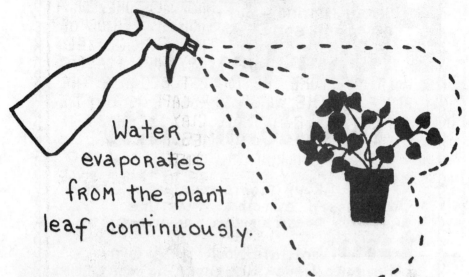

Water
evaporates
from the plant
leaf continuously.

This water lost into the
air is called Transpiration.

The higher the room temperature,
the more water your plants give off.

If you spray mist your plants,
they will love it
and require less frequent waterings.

In addition to SPRAY MISTING – but not instead of – here are some

Other Ways to Provide humidity

one: GROUP plants together and they will absorb each other's MOISTURE. GROUPING DOESN'T MEAN CROWDING.

two: Ventilate YOUR home with fresh air. Generally, THERE is MORE MOISTURE OUTDOORS THAN INDOORS.

three: Take advantage of places with high humidity. Keep plants in bathrooms, and above sinks, dishwashers and washing machines.

four: Place cans of water on top of, near, or hanging from heaters. This humidity will help everyone.

five: Set plates or jars of water around plants.

Six: Rest plants over wells of water. Water wells surround plants with evaporating water.

a **Water Well**, sometimes called
a dry well, consists of TWO parts:
1. Well pot
2. a. well perch
   b. dish or
   c. Rest.

the well pot can be any container that is Rustproof. We have
used such things as

Glass baking dishes, bowls,
old funky Roasting pans,
Decorative cachepots,
Cafeteria Trays, plates
and Recycled containers

to make handsome and practical
water wells. ♥ Be Creative ♥
and allow your plants and sur-
roundings to inspire you to create
an original way of humidifying
your home.

A. Perch Method – especially
GOOD FOR plants you might
ordinarily hang. Instead of
hanging them, set the plants on
top of tall perches that will give
their foliage ROOM TO hang.

perch

well pot — water

① Place a perch
(ROCK, brick, mug,
upside–down clay
pot, saucer or bowl)
in the well pot.
② Set your plant
on top of the perch.
③ Add ¼ inch of
water in the well pot.

Everytime you water your plant, the
excess will run into the well pot,
replenishing the water supply.

B. Double Dish Method – best for
bottom watering.

Well Pot

Water

① Set a dish (right–
side up) into the
well pot, under the
plant pot.
② Put water around
the dish, in the well
pot.
This method is
especially GOOD FOR VIOLETS and all
other plants you frequently fertilize.

C Resting Method – also uses

Run-off water to humidify your plants. This is the easiest method to use when housing several plants in one area.

① Place 1-2 inches of shells, sand, or pebbles into the bottom of the well pot. We like to break up and use our favorite broken china and pottery.

② Set your plants on top of this Rest and fill with about ¼ inch of water.

water level

Be sure the bottom of the pot does not sit in water, because the plants could drink up too much water and then suffocate from the lack of oxygen.

Useful tips

1. Add several chips of fireplace charcoal to the well water. The charcoal helps to keep the water fresh and sweet.

2. To prevent mold, frequently let your water wells dry out. Take them apart and wash them occasionally.

3. Water wells are life savers for plants with vacationing parents.

4. Succulent plants (jade, cacti, geraniums, etc.) do not need wells because they retain a great deal of water. Too much moisture can rot these plants.

5. We have found that using water wells increases the quality of plant growth and lessens the upkeep (our plants require less frequent waterings.)

Water

Good water is fresh, clean & tepid (room temperature/warm). Spring, bottled, well & rain waters are good. If you live in the city like us, try our special trick! We fill a bucket with tap water & let it rest overnight. By morning, the water is room temperature, the chlorine has evaporated & many of the impurities have settled to the bottom. We ladle the water out to the thirsty plants, throwing out the last few inches of impure water.

HOW TO WATER YOUR PLANTS

THERE ARE SEVERAL WAYS YOU CAN WATER YOUR PLANTS... WE USE THEM ALL.

1. TOP WATER - WATER FROM THE TOP, MAKING SURE WATER COMES OUT THE DRAINAGE HOLE. IT'S GOOD TO FILL THE POT AND LET DRAIN SEVERAL TIMES FOR THOROUGH WATERING. IF YOU HAVE A POT WITHOUT A DRAINAGE HOLE, BE CAREFUL NOT TO FLOAT YOUR PLANT.

2. BOTTOM WATER - PUT WATER IN THE DISH UNDER DRAINAGE HOLE. THE PLANT WILL DRINK THE AMOUNT IT WANTS IN ½ HOUR. REFILL DISH IF NECESSARY. WATER THIS WAY IF YOU THINK TOP WATERING MIGHT DISTURB PLANTS OR SEEDS.

3. SUBMERGE METHOD - STAND UNGLAZED CLAY POTS IN TUB OR SINK, WITH WATER LEVEL UP TO TOP OF POTS. REMOVE AFTER 15 min. THIS IS GOOD TO DO IN THE WINTER AFTER LETTING YOUR PLANTS DRY OUT. BY THIS METHOD, WATER PENETRATES THE SOIL EVENLY, PREVENTING WATER CANALS, p.24.

DRAINAGE

GOOD DRAINAGE IS ABSOLUTELY NECESSARY FOR A HEALTHY PLANT. SOGGY SOIL WILL SUFFOCATE AND ROT YOUR PLANT. HERE IS WHAT YOU CAN DO TO YOUR POT TO INSURE GOOD DRAINAGE.

CLAY POTS (UNGLAZED)

LAY ONE PIECE OF BROKEN POTTERY IN THE BOTTOM OVER THE HOLE TO PREVENT LOSS OF SOIL. FREQUENTLY AERATE SOIL (p.25).

CLAY POTS (GLAZED) PLASTIC POTS and ALL CONTAINERS WITHOUT DRAINAGE HOLES.

LAY SEVERAL LAYERS OF BROKEN POTTERY IN THE BOTTOM. THIS WILL ABSORB ANY EXCESS WATER. COVER THIS WITH ABOUT ½" OF CHARCOAL. THIS ACTS AS A WATER FILTER AND WILL KEEP THE SOIL FRESH. EVEN WITH THIS LAYERING ~ WATERING SHOULD STILL BE DONE WITH EXTRA CARE.

Preventing Water Problems

If water sits on the top of the soil, your soil could be compacted. Re-pot your plant because the soil is so bad the water cannot get through.

If water runs quickly through the pot, your soil probably has water canals, caused by the water pushing away the less-dense soil particles, and then following the same widening path each time you water. This process keeps the soil from becoming evenly moist. ...... Water canals can be prevented if you periodically <u>aerate</u> your soil.

To <u>AERATE</u>: gently loosen the top inch of soil by lifting it with a fork. This will permit ⓐ the passage of air to the roots and ⓑ even and thorough watering.

WE RECOMMEND:

① USING TEPID WATER BECAUSE COLD WATER CAN SHOCK ROOTS AND CAUSE SPOTS ON LEAVES.

② LETTING THE WATER STAND OVERNIGHT — ALLOWING THE CHEMICALS TO SETTLE — and NOT USING THE LAST BIT IN THE BOTTOM OF THE WATERING can.

③ USING RAIN WATER.

④ MAKING SURE YOUR SOIL IS MOIST, NOT SOGGY. ROOTS KEPT IN SOGGY SOIL ACTUALLY SUFFOCATE FROM LACK OF OXYGEN. POTS SHOULD NEVER SIT IN SAUCERS OF EXCESS WATER FOR OVER 30 minutes.

DO YOU THINK YOUR PLANT NEEDS REPOTTING?

① Is it potbound? Potbound means that the roots are jammed in the pot and growing out of the bottom hole.

② Is the soil old? p.35.

③ Are there critters in the soil? Generally you will see them "swim" around when you water.

④ Does your plant seem crowded? Comfort is a pot that is not too big and not too small. If the pot is too large there will be aeration problems and the roots will grow like crazy and the foliage will grow like same. Too small can crowd.

⑤ The plant's soil should look fresh, clean, dark, loose, & rich. If it doesn't it probably isn't.

⑥ Is there a change in the season? Is your plant drying out too fast or staying wet too long?

⑦ Has the foliage recently been trimmed drastically? If so, the root system should be pruned to proportion. 26

⑧ Is the pot 20 times larger than the plant?
Did you answer yes?..Proceed!

PREPARATION

Pick your pot. Generally you will want to use a pot just one size larger than the pot the plant is in now. Do not feel obligated to change pot size every time. Depending on the size root structure, you may feel right about putting the plant back in the same pot. Scrub the old pot to get rid of the collected yuck. You will also need an old knife and some soil.

HOW TO REPOT 1,2,3

1 With an old knife, "run" around the edge of the pot, then tap the pot on the side. Generally it is easiest to remove a plant when the soil is dryish. Be ready to catch your plant at the base of the stem as it falls from the pot. Loosen the roots,

27

gently spreading them in all directions. Trim if need be with a sharp knife or scissors. Examine the soil and roots. This is the half you normally cannot see. Take this golden opportunity to look closely. If critters are the problem, you can wash the root gently under a spray nozzle. Use tepid water.

2 Cover the hole of your new pot with broken pottery, & cover that with soil — (judging your space). Add broken pottery and charcoal if your pot has no hole for drainage. Tenderly put in your plant, holding it so the roots are relaxed. Add soil around the edges. You should have 1 to 2 inches of fresh soil around the roots. Tap the pot gently so the soil settles. Water and spray mist clean.

3 Repotting is an experience that you share sort of privately with your plant. Be gentle and confident. All plants are made differently. Plants of the same species generally follow similar

patterns of growth. Grape Ivies
have fine delicate Roots that
Run like small hairs meshing
the soil. Spider plants have
strong solid firm Roots that curl
up like snakes. Enjoy what you
see and clean up your mess.
IT is
that
simple.

○ COMPOST ○
making your own soil

Creating your own soil, composting, is the wonder of organic gardening. \This\ is the finest soil with which to house your plants. It is working with nature to make a special supply of soil, just for you and your plants.

In nature, compost is the natural way of renewing the earth's fertility. The forest floor is covered with compost created by the natural decay of all the leaves, trees and wildlife that have fallen there. The resulting humus nourishes the living plants, and is one of the beautiful examples of eternal life.

Making your own compost can be as simple or as complex as you wish to make it. The object is to simply rescue the organic waste that is now going into the garbage. It is piled outdoors and then left for mother nature to perform the miracle of transforming it into nourishing soil.

Naturally, the more you learn about composting, the better the end result will be. But... don't be put off by the thousands of words written on the subject. Just remember that any organic matter that is dead is going to eventually turn into humus whether you do anything about it or not, so you might as well start collecting it in one spot and have your own supply of nature's best!

30

a good basic recipe for a bugless and odorless compost is:

¼ Garden or packaged (apartment dwellers) soil

¼ Grass, leaves, peatmoss, straw, hay, clippings

¼ Fresh or rotted manure chicken/horse/cow/rabbit

¼ Kitchen waste - fruit and vegetable peels, cores, tops and seeds, crushed egg shells, coffee grounds, tea leaves, chicken bones, and leftover-leftovers!

ORGANIC MATTER

Layer these 1-3 inches as you go. Keep moist (not soggy). It takes from 3-6 months to completely decompose to rich, beautiful soil. You will know when it's ready!

31

In choosing the spot, make it as handy as possible. Here are two ways we like to compost.

ONE
Dig a hole about 4'x6'x2' and pile the soil to one side. If this already sounds like too much work, forget it and start on the top of the ground. The big advantage of the hole is that it confines the garbage and gives you a ready supply of soil to use for layering as you go along.

LEAVES
SOIL
GARBAGE
GRASS
GARBAGE
MANURE

Heat

TWO
Punch holes in the bottom (from the inside-out) of a trash can. Lay three to four inches of straw or gravel in the bottom for drainage. Set the can on several bricks over the ground or tray of some kind to collect the water run-off. Then layer the garbage as you would for a compost pile. When your first can is filled, start composting in another can. This will insure a constant supply of soil.

GRASS
Garbage
MANURE
Leaves
Garbage
MANURE
SOIL   GRASS
GARBAGE
LEAVES
GRAVEL

The organic materials used will of course determine the quality of the finished product and the speed with which it decomposes. Here are some tips on that;

1. Soft materials break down quicker than hard (bone, branches) materials. The liberal use of manure speeds up the decomposition process and adds valuable nitrogen.

2. Stop throwing good nutrients into your garbage. Keep a small pail, old milk carton or dish near your sink for all your organic waste. Take it out daily.

3. Keep a digging tool by the pile so the garbage can easily be covered with manure, soil or clippings each time you take it out.

4. Earthworms will come. They do a great job of mixing, aerating, and breaking down rough, fiberous materials. They will thrive and multiply. Buy them if you need to.

5. Fireplace ashes, hair and vacuum cleaner dirt all go in. A lot of materials are readily available around the house, but you need not stop there. There are many sources of additional materials that are free for the asking. Vegetable markets usually give away their trimmings. Barber shops throw out hair clippings (very rich in potash and phosphoric acid). Get crab and shrimp shells from fish processing plants.

This list could go on and on, but use your own ingenuity. If it's organic, it's good!

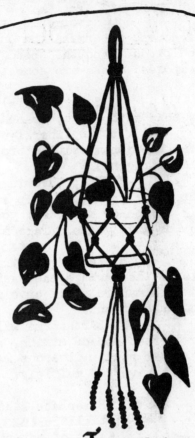

The real joy of
composting comes when you see the
results in the good health and
vigor of your house and garden
plants. Though it takes a little
time and effort, once you get a
compost pile going, chances are
you will become completely absorbed
in mother nature's process of
recycling.

Old Soil

isn't delicious anymore! It lacks nitrogen, phosphorus & potash ... all necessary for **PROPER NUTRITION.** After plants have absorbed these necessary nutrients, we need to fertilize. This way, we replenish the depleted nutrients that our plants need to be strong.

whether you buy **ORGANIC** fertilizers, or compost your own (p.30), they will be gentle to your plants. Organic fertilizers are made from once living plants and animals.

Purchased plant foods have 3 numbers on their labels. These stand for the nutrients:
nitrogen — promotes growth & color of foliage (fish, blood meal & bone meal).
phosphorus — promotes flowers & fruits and strengthens roots (bone meal and ground phosphate rock).
potash — promotes general health (wood ashes from fireplace, kelp).

FOOD FOR THOUGHT

Would you feed your body, for example, salad dressing made from fresh home grown spices, pure olive oil, fresh squeezed lemon juice and fertile eggs (all high in nutrition), or syn-thetic salad dressing made from dehydrated onions, starch, salt, hydrolized vegetable pro-tein, monosodium glutamate, beef fat, spices, polysorbate 60 (improves creaminess), xanthan gum (improves pourability), flavorings, sorbic acid, potassium sorbate and calcium disodium, EDTA added as preservative?

Plants don't like chemical foods either. They prefer natural organic fertilizers that break down slowly, giving them nice meals rather than harsh chemical shocks. Plants don't like to be pushed into quick growth through harsh chemical fertilizers, stimulants, vigorous vitamin doses and extra light. Never given a rest, often they just give up and die.

If you purchase a plant that dies upon arrival it could very well be that it was pushed to death in the nursery. This, unfortunately, is not uncommon. We've seen many nurseries that force their plants to grow as quickly as they can for the most buck. We guess they don't think of plants as individual living things on our planet.

LIGHT

IT'S THE GREEN PLANT CELLS THAT HAVE FOUND A WAY TO CAPTURE AND UTILIZE LIGHT ENERGY TO MAKE FOOD. THE PLANT TAKES IN CARBON DIOXIDE - AND WITH THE ENERGY FROM THE SUN - BREAKS THE BOND BETWEEN THE CARBON AND THE OXYGEN, IT USES THE CARBON TO MAKE FOOD, AND GIVES OFF THE OXYGEN BACK TO US. SUGAR IS PRODUCED IN THE LEAVES BY THIS PROCESS
(PHOTOSYNTHESIS)
AND IS TRANSPORTED THROUGHOUT THE PLANT, NOURISHING THE LIVING CELLS WITHIN.

IT IS IMPORTANT TO KEEP PLANT LEAVES CLEAN SO THEY MAY ABSORB LIGHT (p. 48)

BRIGHT BUT NOT DIRECT SUN	INDIRECT LIGHT FILTERED THROUGH CURTAIN	LITTLE LIGHT FROM BEHIND TREE

Generally PLANTS WITH WHITE OR COLORFUL LEAVES. Many VARIEGATED VARIETIES. PLANTS KNOWN FOR THEIR BLOOMS. HERBS.	Wandering Jew FERNS CREEPING Charlie PIGGYBACK DRACAENA MOST HOUSEPLANTS	SANSEVERIA GRAPE IVY GOLDEN POTHOS PHILODENDRON KANGAROO (BUT THESE PLANTS PREFER INDIRECT LIGHT)

YOU HAVE PROBABLY NOTICED THAT PLANTS FOLLOW THE SUN. AUXIN, A PLANT HORMONE THAT PROMOTES CELL GROWTH, IS RESPONSIBLE FOR THIS. AUXIN GATHERS IN THE STEM ON THE OPPOSITE SIDE FROM THE LIGHT. THE CELLS ON THIS SIDE GROW FASTER WITH THE HELP OF THE AUXIN & THUS THE STEM MOVES TOWARD THE LIGHT.

IF YOU TURN YOUR PLANT, IT IS GOOD TO GIVE YOUR PLANT A QUARTER TURN EACH DAY SO THAT THE STEM WILL GROW TALL, STRAIGHT & STRONG. IF YOUR PLANT GETS A HALF-TURN EACH DAY, SOME OF THE NEW GROWTH WILL BE WASTED MOVING THE PLANT BACK & FORTH.

YOU DON'T HAVE TO TURN YOUR PLANT AT ALL IF YOU LIKE ITS FUNKY SHAPE!

SUMMER/WINTER

Be alert to seasonal changes and how they affect your houseplants. Different plants need different amounts of light. We are conscious of how our plants react to their light source, and if need be, we move them closer to, or further from, it. Pruning outdoor trees, or changing indoor curtains, can change the temperature and the amount of light that is coming through your window. Seasonal changes can be extreme. Plants are alive and do not like extremes any greater than we do.

WINTER   SUMMER

GETTING READY FOR SUMMER

[1] More light will be coming through your windows. Find new places for those plants that will burn in too much heat or sun. Put cacti, herbs, coleus and other sun lovers in those sunny windows.

[2] Gradually, your plants will need more water because
(A) They are growing more, and
(B) The warmth of the day will dry them out more quickly.

[3] Spray mist with warm water daily. Do not mist in the warmth of the day. Why? Because the water acts like a lens, magnifies the sun's rays & burns the leaves.

[4] Repot any plant that needs it. Are roots coming out of the bottom, or could it be that the soil is bad? P. 26

[5] Begin in March to give your plants organic fish emulsion, as mild as spring.

6 We find it helpful to Repot small plants in small clay pots into plastic or glazed pots. During the summer, small clay pots can need water up to three times a day.

SPECIAL WINTER CARE

1 Prepare for frost by bringing inside those plants that would find winter too harsh. As you bring them inside, be sure to wash well, inspect, and repot. This will give your plants a clean fresh start.

2 Take cuttings from those bedded plants (e.g., coleus, begonias and geraniums etc.) that might frost and that you especially want to save. Rinse the cutting clean in tepid water and then root indoors.

3 Stop fertilizing for three months (December, January, and February). Let your plant rest.

4 Gradually, as your plants go dormant for the winter, you

will notice that they need less watering. Frequently spray mist with tepid water and be very shy about watering the soil itself.

5 Keep leaves and windows clean and curtains open.

6 Remember to give your house, your plants, you and your housemates fresh air every day. Open doors when the day is warm and the breeze is soft.

7 Spray mist during the warmth of the day, (so as not to chill).

8 It is good to repot into clay those plants in plastic, tin, or ceramic. This helps prevent overwatering.

9 Move plants closer to the light; i.e., If you had a grape ivy across the room from the window all summer, you will have to move it closer to the incoming light for the winter.

♥ propagation

There are eight easy ways to propagate in your home!

① Many plants root easily in water as long as at least one node is submerged. Try Coleus, false Aralia, Wandering Jew, golden Pothos and Creeping Charlie. When roots look strong, slips may be planted in soil. Keep the soil extra moist for the first few days. This will make the transition from water to soil easier on the roots.

NODES
GROWING CENTERS

WINE

② If you are rooting several cuttings, try potting in soil and Bottom watering - p. 22 Keep the soil extra moist for about the first three weeks.

MILK

③ Mother-Leaf Method: for piggybacks, gently fold-under the mother leaf and cover with soil. She will nourish her standing babies. Bottom Water.

④ In every seed there is a tiny package of food and a tiny sleeping plant.

If a seed is kept warm and moist, a tiny root reaches down into the soil and a stem shoots up toward the sun.

The young plant lives on the food in the seed until it has grown its first leaves. The leaves then make food for the plant (photosynthesis).

The roots of a plant draw water and minerals out of the soil. The stem takes this water from the roots up to the leaves.

Ⓐ fill container with soil.

Ⓑ Lay in your seed and lightly cover with soil.

Ⓒ Cover container with re-usable plastic wrap. This acts as a greenhouse. Poke a few holes for air circulation.

poke holes in container too!

Ⓓ Set container in a dish or tray for Bottom watering

Ⓔ Keep in a warm place. (on top or near your oven)

Ⓕ When sprout appears, set your new plant in a bright window.

⑤ African Violets — root in water or soil. Roots grow out the bottom of the stem.  water

⑥ Ferns ～ mature ferns produce spores (fern seeds) on the undersides of their fronds. To propagate, lay frond, bottom side down, on top of the soil. If needed, secure to the soil with a wire or a hair pin. Keep moist.

⑦ Spider ～ Lay baby in soil or root by floating baby in water. Plant in soil when roots develop. Some plants can live and even grow in water for up to a year. Add fish emulsion for food.

♡ SICKBAY ♡

Wash your troubles away - or

HOW TO WASH YOUR PLANTS

WHEN YOU SEE SOME SMALL "THINGS" ON A PLANT, IMMEDIATELY WASH IT WELL. RUN IT UNDER TEPID WATER IN A SINK OR TUB. USING SPRAY NOZZLE, WASH AFFECTED AREA WELL. WHEN A PLANT DOES NOT NEED WATERING, LAY IT ON ITS SIDE, SO THAT ONLY THE LEAVES GET WASHED. HOLD THE LEAVES AND SHOWER GENTLY ON UNDERSIDES & STEMS. WASH ALL OTHER PLANTS NEAR IT IN THE SAME FASHION. WASH THE

BUGS off everyday 'till they are Gone! Also spray mist with a light soap solution.

Also important is that a plant with bugs should be isolated (away) from other plants! When a plant is isolated and under-going a water wash treatment for bug removal, it is said to be in sickbay. Sickbay should be an even temperature, morning sun window. Sickbay should be near water to encourage frequent showers. Spray mist to prevent bugs.

We have learned that chemical poisons are not necessary and definitely ridiculous to use or even to have in your home. You need not poison your houseplants.

If badly infested &/or too large to move, use a paper towel & water mixed with a couple of drops of baby shampoo. Wash undersides & tops of leaves & stems. Spray mist with tepid water. Before you start, cover the soil with newspaper. If all else fails- kiss it good-by. ♡

ORGANIC CARE CENTER

♡ BUG LIST ♡

COMMON CRITTERS- WHY & WHAT TO DO

APHiDS

CLEAR GREEN FLIES THAT CLUSTER ON STEMS, UNDER LEAVES &/OR ON NEW GROWTH. OFTEN BROUGHT IN ON CUT FLOWERS.

WHY: YOUR PLANT IS NOT CLEAN

WHAT TO DO: WASH PLANT

EARTHWORMS

CUTE GRAYISH, PINKISH, BLACKISH, SLOW MOVING, HARMLESS 1" TO 3" LONG & THIN

WHY: YOU ARE LUCKY TO FIND THEM IN YOUR SOIL. PROBABLY YOUR SOIL IS VERY RICH & GOOD COMPOST.

WHAT TO DO: LOVE THEM- THEY ARE GOOD FOR THE SOIL. THEY WILL NOT CRAWL OUT. IF YOUR POT IS SMALL MOVE THE WORM OUTSIDE.

MEALYBUG

TEENY TINY WHITE THINGS THAT CLUSTER ON THE UNDERSIDES OF LEAVES & STEMS AND LOOK LIKE FUZZ. HARMFUL.

WHY: YOUR PLANT IS NOT CLEAN

WHAT TO DO: WASH PLANT &/OR APPLY RUBBING ALCOHOL DIRECTLY ONTO BUGS WITH A COTTON BALL —OR— SPRAY ENTIRE PLANT WITH 1 PART RUBBING ALCOHOL TO 1 PART WATER (COVER SOIL WITH PAPER). AFTER 15 MIN RINSE WITH CLEAR WATER BY SPRAYING TILL DRENCHED. KEEP YOUR OTHER PLANTS CLEAN AND FAR AWAY. IF BUGS OR EGGS ARE IN THE SOIL YOU MUST REPOT & WASH ROOTS.

REDSPIDER

RED DUST AND WEBS ON UNDERSIDE OF LEAVES. SILVER BROWNISH SPOTTED LEAVES. PESTS ARE SUCKING THE NOURISHMENT FROM THE UNDERSIDES OF THE LEAVES.

WHY: YOUR PLANT IS NOT CLEAN

WHAT TO DO: WASH THOROUGHLY KEEP AWAY FROM OTHER PLANTS. IT is possible for some of the branches to be so badly infested that you would choose to cut them rather than wash them. Do not compost what you cut. Spray mist all plants.

SCALE

ovalish brown shell coated insect. There are many varieties of scale. (do not mistake for fern spores)
WHY: your plant is not clean
WHAT TO DO: gently scratch each off with your finger nail or a knife. wash plant thoroughly.

WHITEFLY

they flutter away leaving a sticky surface. Take plant to sickbay!
WHY: your plant is not clean
WHAT TO DO: same as aphids wash plant thoroughly - sickbay -

OTHER CRITTERS

of course there are many other critters but most of them you can simply & gently remove xoxo

♥ SPRAY MIST WITH WATER DAILY ♥

We overheat & suffocate our houses so that the air is
as dry as that on the sahara desert. Spraying is necessary for all plants that naturally grow in a moist climate. It is also very important for washing & inspection, even if your plant is on a WATER well. A clean sprayed plant will stand up on its best behavior and
☆ sparkle.

HOW: ○ fill atomizer with ○ warm water. Spray mist each leaf—front & back—'Til leaves drip.

WHEN: ○ as often as possible ○ mornings are great yet many of us night people have good results spraying at whim.

WHY: ○ spraying gets you more ○ in touch with your plants. It replaces the water lost from transpiration. It promotes beautiful, healthy, lush growth. Your tropical houseplants will love being sprayed with water!

Population Control Ideas

① Check for critters on all new plants & fresh cut flowers before bringing them indoors.

② Keep flies (that carry harmful eggs) outside. Use fly paper inside!

③ Keep leaves free of eggs. You can simply wash away an insect problem before it is even a problem.
- EVERYDAY—spray with tepid water
- EVERY 2 WKS—run under faucet

WHEN INFESTED—wash your plant (p.48)

④ If the population control is out of control, you might try putting the plant outside under a covered porch. The natural eco-system might just take care of the problem for you. Some houseplants do quite well outside if protected from the extremes. If you bring it back in; be sure to keep a special eye on it.

⑤ If none of the above work then — KISS IT GOOD-BYE! xoxo

PLANT REMEDY CHART

Let's face it... There are only so many reactions a plant can have. You must be the judge!

PLANT LOOKS LIKE	WHY?	WHAT TO DO ♡
Leaves: turn limp and yellow, get soft, mushy, fade and drop off. Soil is wet or soggy. Poke finger in soil. Plant could drop dead. Panic!	**TOO MUCH WATER** — Lack of oxygen around roots. PLANT DROWNING	Don't water your plant so much. Put plant in a warmer, drier place. If your container has no hole, lay pot on its side to drain. Aerate.
Yellow & wilted leaves that shrivel, turn crisp and fall off. Soil is dry. Test with finger. Stems dry up. Plant can die of neglect. ♡	**TOO LITTLE WATER** — compacted soil water canals. PLANT THIRSTY	Water & mist more often. Try a dry well. Aerate soil. An underwatered plant will usually perk up within hours after watering.

54

PLANT LOOKS LIKE	WHY?	WHAT TO DO ♡
New growth is leggy & spindly. Lower leaves wilt yellow & die	NOT ENOUGH LIGHT	Move gradually toward better light. You may want to "pinch".
YELLOWED BURNED FADED WILTED LEAVES	TOO MUCH LIGHT ♡SUNBURNED♡	Most house plants do not like direct sun! Diffused light best! Give plant less light. Temporary wilt occurs on warm bright days with soil wet or dry. See • Light • Page 38.
IT'S UNHAPPY! (DOWN)	A plant goes through a certain shock whenever moved to a new environment	GIVE TENDER LOVING CARE. BE PATIENT.♡

55

PLANT LOOKS LIKE	WHY?	WHAT TO DO ♡
LEAVES CAN BURN LEAVES TURN BROWN AT EDGES YELLOW LEAVES PLANT COULD DIE	OVER FED	THE MOST GENTLE WAY IS TO FEED YOUR PLANT ORGANIC FISH EMULSION &/ OR LIQUEFIED SEA-WEED. CHEMICAL FERTILIZERS ARE TOO HARSH FOR LIVING THINGS TO EAT.
IT'S NOT PERKY PLANT SAD NO GLOW LEAVES FADE NO BLOOM ♡	UNDER FED	USE A WEAKER SOLUTION (½ THE RECOMMENDED DOSE), BUT FEED YOUR PLANT MORE OFTEN (WEEKLY) – THIS SAVES SHOCKING YOUR PLANT.

PLANT LOOKS LIKE	WHY?	WHAT TO DO ♡
LEAVES CRACK & DRY. FOLIAGE BURNS AT THE TIPS. PLANT LACKS LUSTER!	NOT ENOUGH HUMIDITY PLANTS NEED FRESH AIR	SPRAY MIST OFTEN. TRY A DRY WELL. KEEP PLANTS AWAY FROM HEATERS & OVENS.
PLANT BREAKS OFF AT Soil Level	TOO MUCH WATER POOR DRAINAGE Soil LEVEL TOO HIGH	CUT OFF ROTTED PART AT THE CROWN AND RE-ROOT IT. P.44
CALADIUM "DROPS DEAD"	HAS NOT ACTUALLY DROPPED DEAD IT'S TUBEROUS	CUT BACK AND STORE IN A DARK PLACE UNTIL FEB-APRIL
PLANT FELL OVER ooops	HUMAN ANIMAL WIND	REPOT ♡ IMMEDIATELY

SPROUTS ARE GOOD

T.M.

♥EDIBLE HOUSEPLANTS♥
THAT PROVIDE FRESH,
NUTRITIOUS FOOD IN
3-4 DAYS

THEY ARE CONSIDERED TO BE A GOOD
SOURCE OF VITAMINS & MINERALS.

SPROUTS ARE THE FRESHEST FOOD
YOU CAN EAT BECAUSE THEY ARE
GROWING AS YOU BITE INTO
THEIR LITTLE BODIES.

SCREW
ON
LID

Jar

SCREEN OR
CHEESECLOTH

YOU CAN SPROUT

seeds, whole Grains and dried beans and Peas.

 START ♪

 SPROUTS are GOOD

T.M.

♡ HOW TO SPROUT ♡

SUNDAY NIGHT
SOAK SEED
over night
8-10 HOURS
(Remove
HARD OR
BROKEN SEED)

COVER
WITH MORE
THAN TWICE
THE WATER

2-3 TAB.   ¼ - ⅓ CUP
alfalfa   LENTILS
RADISH   SUNFLOWER
CLOVER   WHEAT
azuki   GARBANZO

Some seeds are unnecessarily treated with chemicals. Only use untreated seed!

🍀~ easy- FUN- CRUNCHY

 (59)

MONDAY DAY

A.M.
of FIRST DAY
of GROWTH—
DRAIN off WATER
then

Rinse ♡ 3 Times

TRIPLE RINSE

WATER 8 SWIM SPROUTS

OUT — IN — OUT — IN

Rubbing vegetable oil on the inside of the ring may prevent the ring from leaving a residue on the screen. If a residue appears, scrub with steel wool.

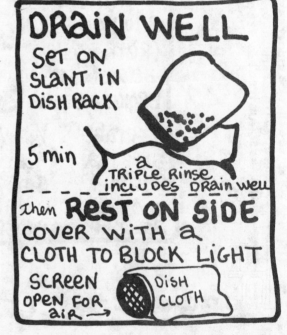

DRAIN WELL
SET ON SLANT IN DISH RACK

5 min

a TRIPLE RINSE INCLUDES DRAIN WELL

then **REST ON SIDE** COVER WITH a CLOTH TO BLOCK LIGHT

SCREEN OPEN FOR air →

DISH CLOTH

SPROUTS are economical because one pound of seed will PRODUCE 6-8 pounds of living food.

Best of all — you can have a fun and easy vegetable Garden in YOUR kitchen (hydroponically) all year around.

LeaVe CoVeReD ON SiNK BoaRD aLL DaY

MONDaY niGHT P.M. Rinse SPROUTS 3 Times

TRiPLe Rinse

COVER SPROUTS FOR niGHT

DRAiN WELL!

Taste your growing sprouts along the way to see when you Like them best. Taste the changes they go through.

61

Sprouts can turn bitter if they
Grow too Long, Get too much Light
(chlorophyll), Stay soggy, DRY-UP,
or are crowded - Lacking air.

for about an hour, resoak seeds if
they dry up... and... resoak sprouts to
freshen up.

Grains are best when sprouts are scarcely LONGER than the Grain itself.

most sprouts taste best and are highest in vitamins between 60-80 hours after 1st. soaking.

EGGS / CHEESE

RAW · MILK · SPROUTS

LEFTOVERS

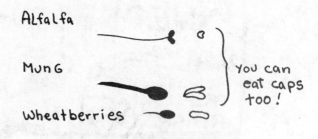

Alfalfa

Mung

Wheatberries

You can eat caps too!

2 DAYS = WHEAT SUNFLOWER

3-4 DAYS = ALL OTHER

GOURMET TREAT

SPROUTS ARE GOOD TO EAT.....

EAT THEM RAW in SALADS, SANDWICHES AND GARNISHES

and

SAUTÉ THEM LIGHTLY WITH VEGETABLES, NUTS AND SEEDS

and

ADD THEM (LAST MINUTE) TO SOUPS, CASSEROLES & SCRAMBLED EGGS

  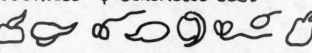

economical

SPROUTS ARE GOOD...

Save sprout Rinsing water
for watering your houseplants.

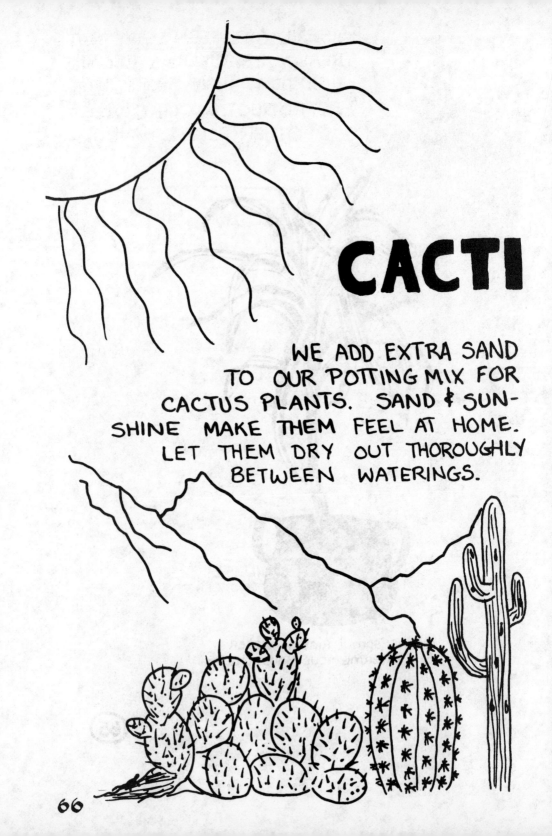

CACTI

WE ADD EXTRA SAND
TO OUR POTTING MIX FOR
CACTUS PLANTS. SAND & SUN-
SHINE MAKE THEM FEEL AT HOME.
LET THEM DRY OUT THOROUGHLY
BETWEEN WATERINGS.

ASPARAGUS FERNS ARE NOT
REALLY TRUE FERNS BECAUSE
THEY DON'T HAVE SPORES FOR
REPRODUCTION LIKE ALL
OTHER FERNS HAVE.

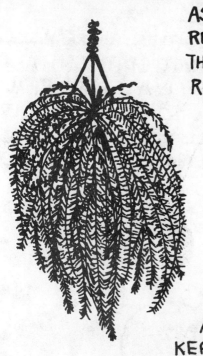

FERNS

FERNS ARE VERY LOVELY
AND HARDY IF THEY ARE
KEPT IN A VERY BRIGHT,
COOLISH, WELL VENTILATED
ROOM. SPRAY MIST EACH FROND
OFTEN WITH WARM WATER. KEEP
FERNS IN CLAY POTS & KEEP THE SOIL
MOIST (NOT SOGGY).   STAND BACK,
WATCH, AND GIVE THEM ROOM TO GROW.
KEEP DYING FRONDS TRIMMED WITH
VERY SHARP SCISSORS. REMEMBER, FERNS
GROW NATURALLY IN RAIN FORESTS.

YOU CAN SIMULATE THIS REFRESHING
RAIN BY GIVING YOUR POTTED PLANT A
COMPLETE SHOWER AT WATERING TIME
USING TEPID WATER. YOU CAN SHOWER
ALL YOUR TROPICAL
PLANTS THIS WAY, TOO.

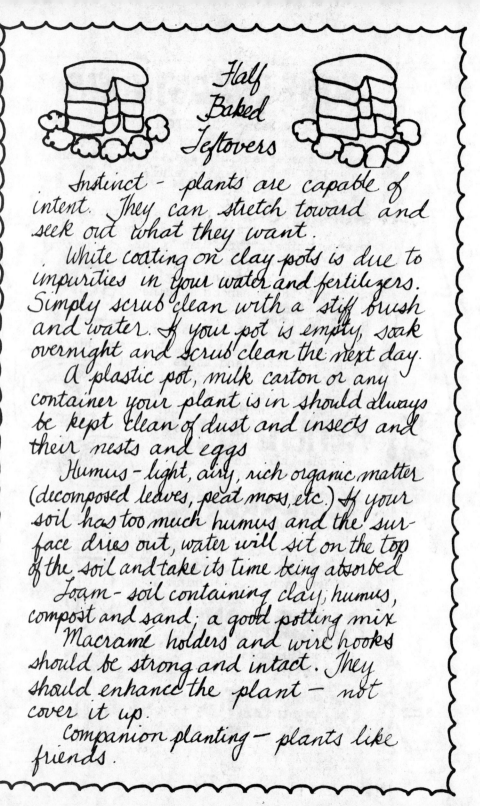

Half Baked Leftovers

Instinct — plants are capable of intent. They can stretch toward and seek out what they want.

White coating on clay pots is due to impurities in your water and fertilizers. Simply scrub clean with a stiff brush and water. If your pot is empty, soak overnight and scrub clean the next day.

A plastic pot, milk carton or any container your plant is in should always be kept clean of dust and insects and their nests and eggs

Humus — light, airy, rich organic matter (decomposed leaves, peat moss, etc.) If your soil has too much humus and the surface dries out, water will sit on the top of the soil and take its time being absorbed

Loam — soil containing clay, humus, compost and sand; a good potting mix

Macramé holders and wire hooks should be strong and intact. They should enhance the plant — not cover it up.

Companion planting — plants like friends.

69

SOME ECOLOGY IDEAS

Being ECOLOGICAL is a lot more than voting every six months for conservation measures; it's a daily commitment to TRY not to be wasteful. Being Ecological is;

LOOKING
at things before throwing them out. Is there a friend, plant, animal, thrift shop, or recycling center that may want what you are throwing away? Someone's TRASH can be someone else's TREASURE.

LOOKING
at things carefully before purchasing them and deciding right then and there what exactly you plan to do with the wrapper or container when finished with the product.

REMEMBERING
to reuse plastic bags. If you insist on plastic, reuse it !

REMEMBERING
not to take paper bags unless you really need them. A lot of purchases can be paid for and carried out without a bag...or bring a bag from your supply at home.

PURCHASING
only returnable bottles. It is absurd that non-returnables still exist in our world.

RECYCLING
to thrift shops what recycling centers cannot take.

REFUSING

to purchase aerosol cans because ① the spray is so fine that our noses cannot filter out the minute particles in the spray, ② the aerosol propellant gas is dangerous to our ozone and ③ what can you do with an empty spray can??????????????

air/SKY/LUNGS
say YUCK

GROWING
YOUR OWN FOODS

SHARING
leftovers with friends!

Something you've eaten for two days could be a fresh treat for someone else. Give a friend a night off from cooking.

PURCHASING

only natural, un-processed foods to help encourage food manufacturers to make their foods wholesome. They will make what we buy!!!!!

plastic cheese PRODUCT

Real Live food

TAKING

unwanted newspapers, bottles, jars, cans, cardboard, junk metals, repairable discards and whatever else your local recycling center can take. This helps them stay in business.

glass   Tin   Paper

LEAVING

Forest plants and mulch right where they grow. If everyone removed our forest plants, we would no longer have forests.

SACRIFICING
the convenience of plastic wrap and foil. If you must use foil or plastic, wash and reuse it many times.

USING
degradable soaps.

yummy

CUTTING DOWN

on all paper products. Buy only natural or white papers. The colored products contain dyes that pollute our waters. (they make the $ go up too.)

PRACTICING ZERO POPULATION GROWTH

(one child or less per person) The population problem is everyone's problem!!!!! Over-population is the basis for all our ecological problems. If you want to have more children than you know what to do with...ADOPT!!

COMPOSTING

everything that decomposes, p 30 .

PURCHASING

recycled items instead of new things whenever possible. Reuse the things already on this planet.

SAVING

electrical energy - cutting ~~down on~~ out on electric can openers, electric knives, electric rollers, electric garbage compactors.

PEDALING

whenever you can! Driving only when you have to and then - only driving economical cars. If everyone did this, our air pollution would be cut in half...Really!!!!!

GROWING

plants indoors and outdoors and taking care of them and the space around you.

REMEMBERING

that the dump is a part of this planet too!

aiR/SKY —— Plants aRE essen-
tial for human Survival. They
give us oxygen to breathe and
food to eat. Without them, our earth
would not be fit for human life.
We feel our green friends
deserve Respect.

PLANT WORDS

AIR ~ all plants need air. they hate cigarette & cigar smoke, aerosols & smog.

ANNUAL ~ lives one year.

BABY SHAMPOO ~ mild soap

CHARCOAL ~ a great purifier keeps water "fresh". prevents stale odor. buy art charcoal sticks or plant charcoal but never use charcoals that have been treated for cooking.

CHEMICAL ROOT STIM-ULANTS ~ they are not necessary.

CUTTING ~ a piece of the plant removed for the purpose of using it to grow another plant (propagation).

DORMANT ~ resting, sleeping.

DRINK ~ fill the pot with water and let it drain. **BIG DRINK** ~ fill the pot with water and let it drain. do this several times.

EGG WATER - Fill a jar with egg shells and water. Allow the water to sit for at least 24 hours. Then use it to give your plant a super treat. Re-use shells 1/2 dozen times.

LARGE PLANTS - Generally easier to care for because they are strong and established.

LIFE STYLE - Raising plants is a wonderful thing to do. Trade cuttings with friends and raise them to trade again.

use the seeds from your

ORIGINAL - That is what all plants are and they should be cared for according to their individual needs.

PERENNIAL - lives many years

PINCHING - cutting your plant for shaping (making it bushier) and/or propagation (p. 44). simply cut off the flowers or growing tips.

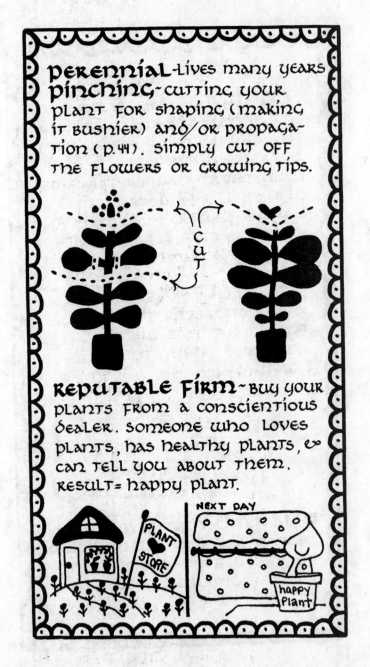

REPUTABLE FIRM - buy your plants from a conscientious dealer. someone who loves plants, has healthy plants, & can tell you about them. RESULT = happy plant.

MUSIC ♪♪♪ PLANTS LOVE IT. THEY PREFER IT LIVE.
RUSTY NAIL TRICK ~ PUT A RUSTY NAIL IN COLEUS SOIL FOR BRIGHTER COLORS.
SMALL PLANTS ~ NEED NURSING AT FIRST ~ LOTS OF FUN!
TEMPERATURE ~ PLANTS HATE DRAFTS, GAS HEATERS, HEATERS IN GENERAL, AND ICY WINDOWS.
TEPID ~ ROOM TEMPERATURE, LUKEWARM, WARM
TOOLS

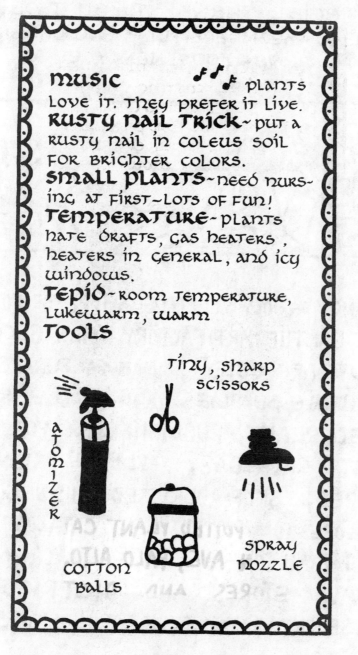

TINY, SHARP SCISSORS

ATOMIZER

COTTON BALLS

SPRAY NOZZLE

♡A SPECIAL THANKS TO ALL THOSE WHO HAVE BEEN HELPFUL & ENCOURAGING. xoxo LOVE-JODY, NANCY, ET AL.

NANCY & JODY'S LITTLE SHOP, THE POTTED PLANT IN THE ARTIFACTORY, HAS BECOME SPROUTS ARE GOOD™, MANUFACTURERS OF SPROUTING SUPPLIES, AND WILD HORSES POTTED PLANT, PUBLISHERS. FOR THE LATEST CATALOGS, PLEASE SEND A STAMPED, SELF-ADDRESSED, BUSINESS-SIZED ENVELOPE TO: POTTED PLANT CATALOG DEPT., 226 HAMILTON CA 94301 U.S.A.. STORES AND DISTRIBUTORS PLEASE INDICATE TYPE OF BUSINESS. ♡